AGE OF DINOSAURS: PTERODACTYL

AGE OF DINOSAURS:

Pterodactyl

SHERYL PETERSON

CREATIVE PAPER BACKS

Published by Creative Paperbacks
P.O. Box 227, Mankato, Minnesota 56002
Creative Paperbacks is an imprint of The Creative Company
www.thecreativecompany.us

Design and production by Blue Design
Art direction by Rita Marshall
Printed by Corporate Graphics in the United States of America

Photographs by Alamy (Blickwinkel, Imagebroker, Interfoto, Pictorial Press Ltd), Bridgeman Art Library (English School), Corbis (Jonathan Blair), Dreamstime (Clearviewstock), Getty Images (DEA Picture Library, Ken Lucas), iStockphoto (Pete Karas), Library of Congress, Sarah Yakawonis/Blue Design

The Library of Congress has cataloged the hardcover edition as follows:
Peterson, Sheryl.
Pterodactyl / by Sheryl Peterson.
p. cm. — (Age of dinosaurs)
Summary: An introduction to the life and era of the flying contemporaries of dinosaurs known as pterodactyls, starting with the creatures' 1784 discovery and ending with present-day research topics.
Includes bibliographical references and index.
ISBN 978-1-58341-975-5 (hardcover)
ISBN 978-0-89812-540-5 (pbk)
1. Pterodactyls—Juvenile literature. I. Title. II. Series.

QE862.P7P48 2010
567.918—dc22   2009025175

CPSIA: 120109 P01089
First Edition
9 8 7 6 5 4 3 2 1

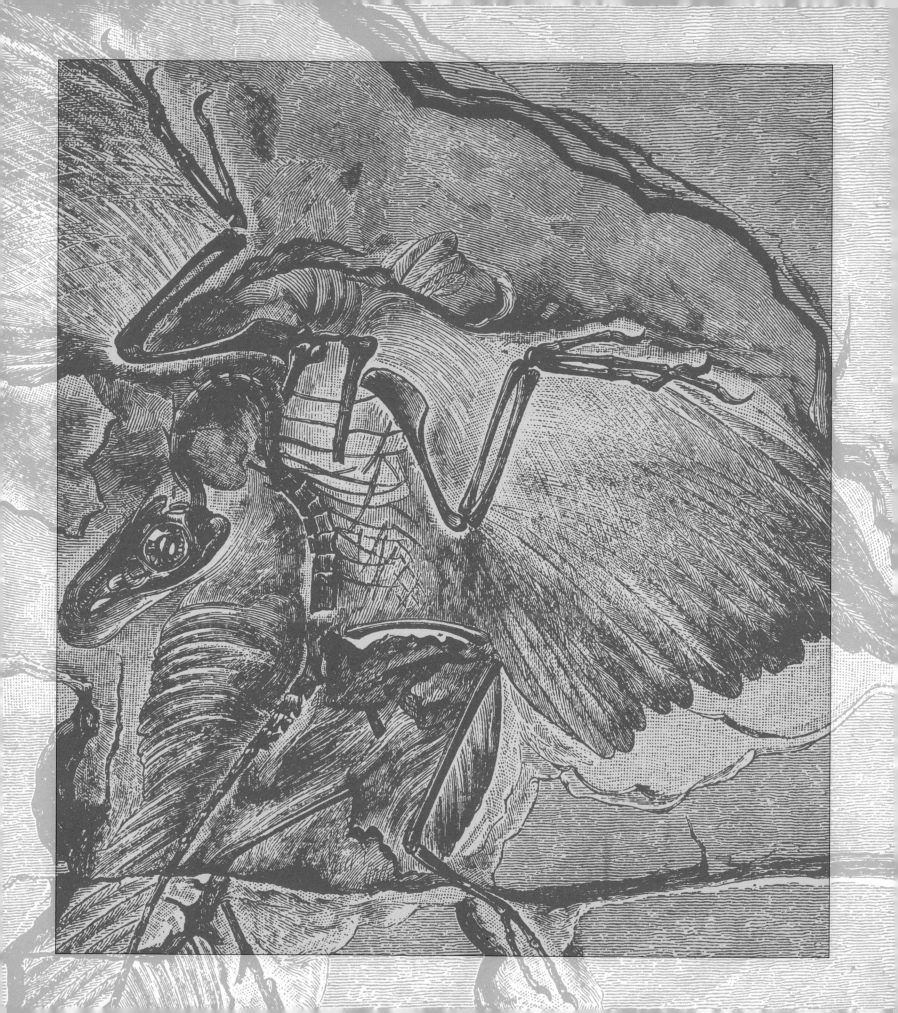

CONTENTS

PTERODACTYL TALES

MYSTERIOUS FLYING REPTILE

Millions of years ago, the salty Jurassic seas covered much of the earth. In the shallow bottoms behind reefs, soft carbonate mud accumulated. Many creatures that fell into the mud or were washed into it from the ocean became stuck. As the mud hardened and turned into limestone, the bodies of horseshoe crabs, shrimps, and insects were eventually buried. Every so often, a small leather-winged creature would also become trapped, with the limestone perfectly preserving the details of its skeleton.

In 1784, workers in the Solnhofen rock quarry in Bavaria, a region of southern Germany, chiseled out slabs of limestone for roofing material. Cutting the stone with picks and small hoes was slow, difficult work, but chipping and scraping alongside the laborers was an Italian scientist named Cosimo Alessandro Collini. He was the **curator** of a private nature cabinet in the palace of Karl Theodor, Elector of Bavaria. (The "cabinet" was akin to today's natural history museums.) Collini patiently picked and dug and searched for signs of prehistoric animal life embedded in the rock. One day, while sweeping off a slab of dusty limestone, he discovered an imprint of a baffling, winged skeleton.

Was it a bat or a strange type of bird? Perhaps it was a miniature dragon! Collini was puzzled by the unusual skeleton preserved in the rock. The scientist did not recognize the specimen as a flying animal,

At the time the first pterosaur fossil was discovered, it was difficult to picture the type of animal that had left such an imprint behind.

so Collini wondered if it might be a mysterious sea creature instead. Since this animal was the first pterosaur to be discovered, Collini had nothing with which he could compare it.

Other scientists at the time thought the fossil belonged to an animal that was half-bird and half-bat. Little did they know that the newly discovered creature had lived 75 million years before birds and 150 million years before bats. The strange discovery was stored on a shelf in the nature cabinet in Mannheim, Germany, for nearly a quarter of a century.

During this time, the Napoleonic Wars were being fought across Europe. The French, led by General Napoleon Bonaparte (who later became emperor), were invading many countries in attempts to take control over as many governments as possible. To protect it from being stolen by plundering armies, Collini's raven-sized fossil was taken to Paris, France, in 1809. It was then delivered to the skilled French **anatomist** Baron Georges Cuvier for safekeeping and study.

Cuvier speculated that the bones came from a type of **reptile** and also noted that the creature's fourth finger was very long. He sketched a birdlike beast with a large head and batlike wing membranes that attached to a single, long finger on each side of the body and named the animal *Ptero-Dactyle,* or "winged-finger." By examining the animal's small teeth set in long jaws, Cuvier determined that it was neither bat nor bird but was more closely related to crocodiles than to any other living family. He called it a "flying reptile," yet that seemed incorrect to most people, since reptiles were usually limited

Baron Georges Cuvier

The man who named *Pterodactylus* possessed one of the finest scientific minds in history. Georges Cuvier was a French vertebrate zoologist and anatomist who is called the "Father of **Paleontology**." Cuvier was born in 1769 and became interested in the sciences at an early age. He revolutionized anatomy by developing a system of classifying animals into four groups based on their skeletal structure, and it was said that Cuvier could reconstruct a skeleton based on a single bone. A great scientific advancement occurred when Cuvier put forth his theories about extinction events. He believed that the earth was extremely old (but not as old as is now known), and that natural events such as catastrophic floods occurred, eliminating certain animal species forever. Cuvier believed that "animals have certain fixed and natural characters," and he determined that any similarities between organisms were due to common functions, not common ancestry. Still, the anatomist's new classification system brought scientists closer to understanding why animals have different structures. Cuvier's influence is commemorated in the names of many animals, including Cuvier's gazelle, Cuvier's toucan, and Cuvier's beaked whale.

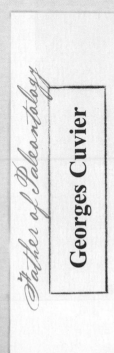

Father of Paleontology

Georges Cuvier

Solnhofen Treasures

Solnhofen is a town in southern Bavaria that gives its name to the limestone found in its vicinity, which began to form in the Jurassic Period, when the area was underwater. Because Solnhofen limestone is fine-grained and pure, it was often quarried for use in making roof and floor tiles from the late 1700s onward. Later, the stone was used in a kind of printing called lithography. Quarry workers were the first to discover fossilized remains that showed what life had been like both above and below the water level in that location millions of years ago. Fossils of pterodactyls, fish, turtles, jellyfish, and worms have been found, along with *Archaeopteryx*, the first primitive bird with feathered wings, and a tiny carnivorous dinosaur called *Compsognathus*. The only dinosaur found at Solnhofen, *Compsognathus* might have hunted for small reptiles and insects or perhaps a river carried its dead body to the lagoon, where it sank and became a fossil. The Bürgermeister Müller Museum, founded in Solnhofen in 1954, houses the quarry's large collection of treasures, including a plaster cast of *Archaeopteryx*.

to movement on the ground. Cuvier's term *Ptero-Dactyle* later took on the Latin form *Pterodactylus* and became the name for all similar **species** of pterosaur.

From then on, pterodactyl became the name commonly applied not only to the genus *Pterodactylus* but to all pterosaurs of the order Pterosauria. The group was known as "winged lizards," since over millions of years, they represented a class of reptiles called Sauropsida that lacked scales but possessed the ability to fly. The earliest pterosaurs appeared in the Late Triassic Period, about 220 million years ago, at approximately the same time as the first dinosaurs. They lived on through the Jurassic Period until the very end of the Cretaceous (about 65 million years ago).

It was not until 1817 that a second specimen of *Pterodactylus* was uncovered, once again from the Solnhofen quarries. Because these specimens were found in an area that had been a prehistoric sea, the idea that pterodactyls were water animals persisted among a small group of scientists as late as the 1830s. German zoologist Johann Georg Wagler even published an 1830 text on amphibians such as frogs and salamanders that showed a pterosaur using its wings as flippers.

Besides their wings, scientists noticed something else interesting about pterodactyls. Their bones had honeycombed air passages

From fossilized remains such as those found at Solnhofen (opposite), artists can render more lifelike images of prehistoric creatures (below).

Sir Richard Owen was well versed in natural history and spent almost 60 years teaching and working at British institutions and museums.

running through them, just like modern birds, which seemed to prove that the animals had been built for flight. Some paleontologists thought pterodactyls could fly to some extent but believed that they were not as capable as today's birds and bats. Others reasoned that the creatures were merely gliders.

In the late 1800s, a debate began between two leading British paleontologists, Richard Owen and Harry Seeley. They argued over whether pterodactyls were cold-blooded reptiles and poor fliers (as Owen believed) or warm-blooded primitive birds (as Seeley thought). The discovery of many more well-preserved pterodactyl fossils helped partially settle the matter. The creatures were proven to be reptiles and not related to birds. But the debate continued as to whether they were warm-blooded and if they had flown.

Since Collini and Cuvier first studied the earliest perplexing fossils, pterodactyl relatives have been found all over the world, from the North American *Pteranodon* to the Chinese *Dsungaripterus* to the South American *Quetzalcoatlus*. Thirty species of pterosaur have been found in the Solnhofen limestone alone. Yet even into the 21st century, pterosaurs continue to mystify scientists and the public.

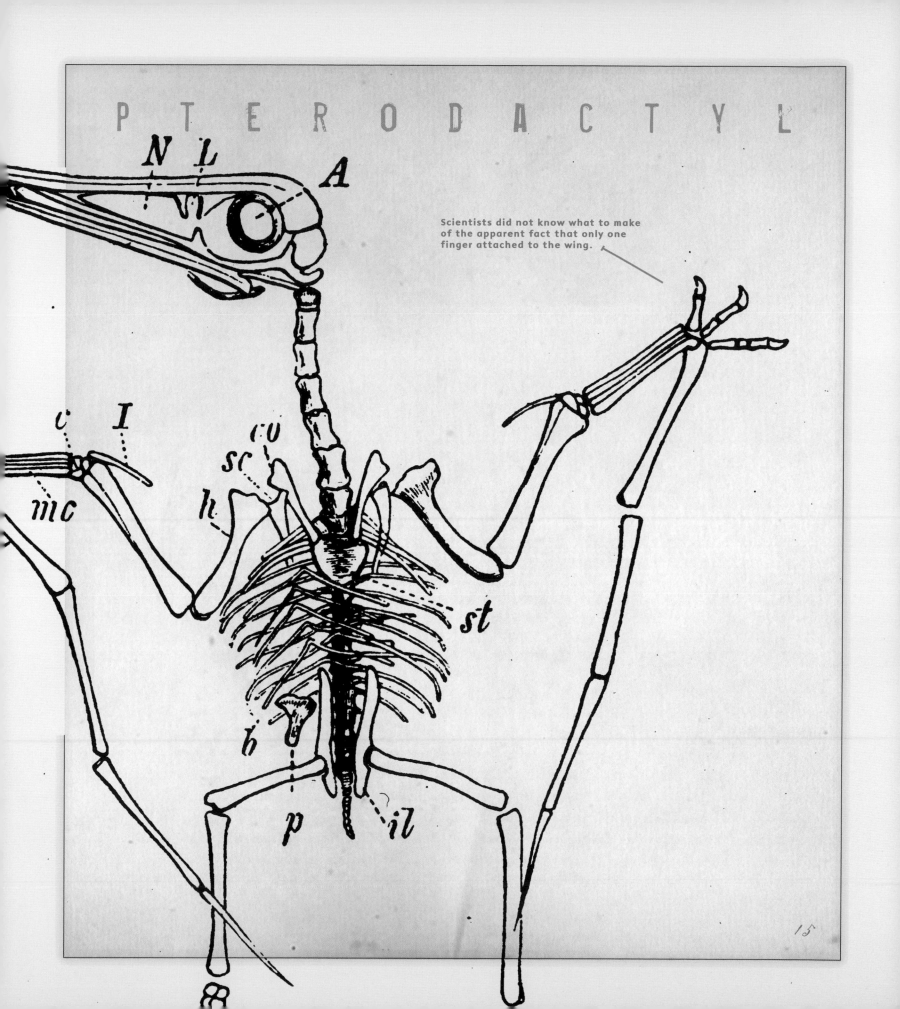

Scientists did not know what to make of the apparent fact that only one finger attached to the wing.

Giant *Quetzalcoatlus*

Quetzalcoatlus is the name of one of the largest flying creatures the world has ever known. This huge, winged North American creature was named after the Aztec feathered-serpent god Quetzalcoatl. Until the 1970s, scientists believed that *Pteranodon*, with its wingspan of up to 30 feet (9 m), was the biggest pterosaur. However, *Quetzalcoatlus*, discovered in 1971, had a wingspan of up to 40 feet (12 m). *Quetzalcoatlus* would have looked like a living aircraft. How could it have flown with such enormous wings? Scientists believe that it must have slowly and deliberately flapped its wings as many large seabirds do today. Once off the ground, it would have been able to soar like an albatross, barely beating its long, narrow wings as it flew over the ocean looking for fish. By the time the dinosaurs and most other prehistoric creatures went extinct about 65 million years ago, *Quetzalcoatlus* had been the only known pterosaur on Earth. Perhaps the gigantic pterosaurs had just gotten too big to live for very long, and as a species, they may have been victims of their own success.

WING-FINGERED FLIER

Dinosaurs may have ruled over the land for 160 million years, but pterodactyls and other winged reptiles ruled the prehistoric skies for just about as long. Some paleontologists say that pterodactyls had many similarities to dinosaurs. They point to such shared physical features as neck joints, jaw joints, small collarbones, and straight ankle hinges as proof.

Pterodactyls were strange creatures that flew over the earth during the Late Jurassic Period (appearing 150 to 145 million years ago) and were very different from flying creatures we know today. Some

Despite its large wingspan and seven-foot-long (2.1 m) legs, *Quetzalcoatlus* had a lightly built, hollow-boned body.

17

earlier reptiles had taken to the air before pterodactyls, but these were strictly gliders. Pterodactyls were probably the first **vertebrates** to achieve self-powered flight by flapping their wings. Some types of pterodactyls were small, about the size of a robin or a crow, with wingspans of only a few inches. Others were as large as today's vultures. Near the end of the Cretaceous Period, enormous relatives of the pterodactyls became common; some, such as *Ornithocheirus*, were as large as small airplanes!

Everything about the genus *Pterodactylus* was long, except for its short tail. It had long wings, a long slender neck, and an elongated head. In some cases, its head was as long as the rest of its body. *Pterodactylus* had long, narrow jaws with powerful muscles and a number of sharp, forward-facing teeth that were designed to grab prey, such as fish, and swallow them whole.

Since *Pterodactylus* was not a bird, it did not have feathers. However, it was covered with short, fine hair that may have provided insulation from the cold. *Pterodactylus* was a relatively small pterosaur, with adult wingspans ranging from 20 to 40 inches (50–102 cm). The animal's hollow bones did not contribute much to its overall weight of 2 to 10 pounds (.91–4.5 kg), enabling it to get off the ground and into the sky. Until recently, some paleontologists had thought that pterodactyls hung upside

Strange Modern Sightings

For thousands of years, people around the world have reported pterodactyl sightings. The appearance of creatures thought to have been extinct for millions of years is an intriguing dilemma. In 1944, a U.S. pilot who was walking through a New Guinea jungle reported seeing a huge animal flying overhead. The man observed what he thought was a gigantic, dark gray bird with a wingspan that seemed to match his Piper airplane's. Giant flying reptiles have also been routinely sighted in Olympic National Park in the American state of Washington. In December 2007, a driver there told police that a pterodactyl caused him to run into a light pole. From the African Congo have come reports of a winged beast that residents call the Kongamoto, or "overwhelmer of boats." In 1925, a man was attacked by a creature and received wounds from its sharp beak. When natives were shown pictures of a pterodactyl, they said it was Kongamoto. Recently, there have been reports of prehistoric birdlike creatures near San Antonio, Texas, where *Quetzalcoatlus* once lived. It does make one wonder.

Could some have survived?

Its large, crested head set the Late Jurassic *Pteranodon* apart
from other pterosaurs; this distinctively winged and toothless
reptile was believed to have flown mainly by soaring.

down from trees like bats and would have needed to drop from a high place in order to gain enough momentum to begin flying. But now most scientists assert that pterodactyls moved around well on land and would have been able to attain flight from the ground.

The arm bones of *Pterodactylus* were long and lightweight. At the end of each arm were three short, clawed fingers and an extremely long fourth finger that reached all the way to the wing tip. This was known as the "wing finger." The wings of *Pterodactylus* were formed by a thin but tough, leathery skin that stretched between its body, the top of its legs, and its elongated fourth fingers. Although five toes were at the end of each leg, the fifth was too small to be of any use. *Pterodactylus* had a very short tail that did not assist in the animal's movement.

For its size, *Pterodactylus* had a relatively large brain inside its 2.4-inch-long (6 cm) skull. Shaped like a double-layered heart, its brain would be comparable to present-day birds of the same size, but it was more developed than other reptiles of similar size. Since flying is a complicated activity, *Pterodactylus* would have required a larger, more advanced brain to control its wings. Flying was the specialty of all pterodactyls, and they could travel much faster and farther than any of the land-based dinosaurs could.

Pterodactyls in general featured large eyes and probably had good vision. This means they would have been able to see across long distances as they flew over the land. Good eyesight would have come in handy while searching for their next meal of fish and would have been necessary to spot danger ahead.

Although pterodactyls and dinosaurs were closely related, they were separate groups of animals. By definition, all dinosaurs moved in an upright stance, while pterodactyls likely had a semi-upright position when walking. While on land, smaller pterodactyls such as *Rhamphorhynchus* and *Pterodactylus* probably moved rather quickly on all four feet. Some pterodactyls such as *Dimorphodon* had longer hind limbs and may have run on two hind legs like modern roadrunners. Although some paleontologists think they could have both walked and flown, pterodactyls were not the same as the birds that lived during prehistoric times, nor were they like the birds we see at our birdfeeders today.

Pterodactyls would have made their homes near a lake or sea, where there was plenty of food available. The **carnivorous** pterodactyl ate fish and other small animals. Flying over a body of water, a pterodactyl would have dipped its beak and opened up its bottom jaw. Scooping up water as it flew, the flying fisher would soon have had a mouthful of tiny, tasty fish. Pterodactyls also dined on **mollusks** and crabs and **scavenged** for dead animals on land. If nothing else was available, a pterodactyl would have dug its beak deep into the beach sand to search for worms and insects.

It has been suggested that some pterosaurs were able to swim much like modern shorebirds. The recent discovery of unusual

Supporting the theories about pterodactyls' similarities to modern bats are illustrations that show the pterosaur in a batlike position such as hanging from a tree.

23

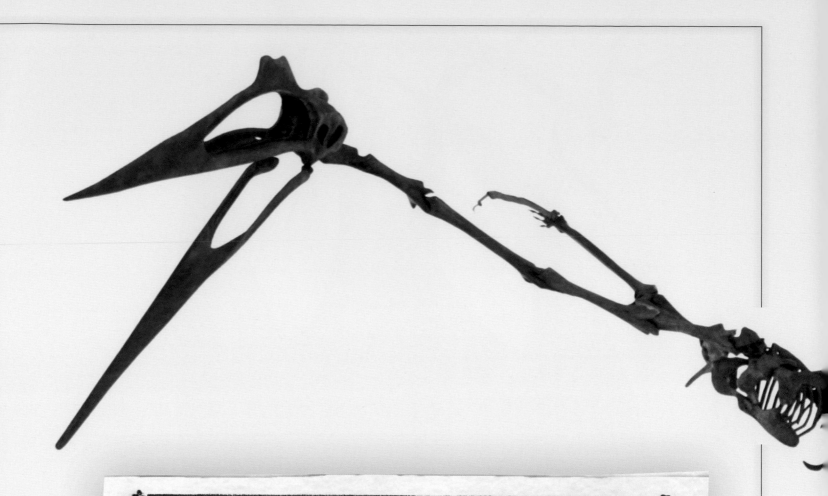

Tiny *Anurognathus*

A pterosaur smaller than a garden sparrow lived at the time of *Pterodactylus*. *Anurognathus*'s body was only about 3.5 inches (9 cm) long, but it had a wingspan of 20 inches (50 cm), or about 6 times its body length. *Anurognathus* means "without tail or jaw." The minute creature survived off of small flying insects such as lacewings and damselflies, catching them with its sturdy beak and needle-like teeth. Scientists speculate that *Anurognathus* lived near large sauropod dinosaurs such as *Diplodocus* and perched on their backs. They may have served a similar purpose as the present-day tick birds that sit on the backs of herd animals, feeding on the insects that the large animals attract. Being up high would have given *Anurognathus* some much-needed protection from predators below, and the bugs that constantly hovered around the skyscraper-sized dinosaurs would have provided a steady source of food. To date, only one fossil of the little creature is known. It was found in 1923 in the Solnhofen limestone quarries in Bavaria. *Anurognathus* is comparable in body size to a present-day hummingbird—but with much bigger, kite-shaped wings.

tracks in the American Southwest that show scrape marks were probably made by a pterodactyl paddling in shallow water. There is, however, no evidence of diving behavior.

Some scientists think pterodactyls had a throat pouch, much like a pelican's. Such a pouch could have been used for storing fish to transport back to a nesting area to feed its young. The baby pterodactyl would have put its beak in the adult's mouth and picked out its meal, piece by piece.

Pterodactyls would have been cautious when building a nest, because some dinosaurs were egg thieves. Two fossilized pterosaur eggs, reported to be about 121 million years old, were discovered in China in 2004. The eggs had a soft, leathery shell similar to that of crocodile and turtle eggs. This gave experts strong evidence that earlier pterodactyls also laid eggs. Since their bodies were not very big, they most likely laid only one or two eggs at a time. Females would not have been able to fly carrying more weight than that.

Another fossilized egg was found in Argentina in 2004. The egg and **embryo** inside it were among fossils of many juvenile and adult remains, suggesting that the winged reptiles lived in groups and protected their young. From what scientists can tell about the advanced development of the fossilized embryo, they reason that the young would have grown up fast and learned to fly quickly.

Some skeletal reconstructions show that early pterodactyls had shorter tails than their later counterparts, and their skulls were crestless.

PTEROSAURS AND DINOSAURS

Pterosaurs were abundant during the Jurassic Period of 208 to 144 million years ago. At that time, the earth was a very different place. Scientists believe that most of Earth's landmasses, now called continents, were once a giant supercontinent called Pangaea. During the 64 million years of the Jurassic, the supercontinent broke into two major fragments—Laurasia in the north and Gondwana in the south. These fragments eventually separated into the seven continents that we know on Earth today. As the continents moved, they collided with pieces of the ocean floor, causing the formation of several mountain ranges around the world—including the Rocky Mountains in North America and the Alps in Europe.

As the landmasses shifted, sea levels rose, and **climates** changed in different parts of the world. Some tropical parts of the world became drier, while other places experienced periods of heavy monsoon rains. Flowering plants had not yet appeared on Earth during the Jurassic, but there were lush jungles full of **conifers**, **ginkgoes**, ferns, and stout, leafy **cycads**. The vast oceans became habitat for marine life forms such as sponges and corals.

Perhaps in response to this change in climate and abundance of food sources, some dinosaur species such as the **herbivores** *Diplodocus* and *Brachiosaurus* became gigantic in size. These dinosaurs were known as sauropods. Also roaming the planet were

Ocean Monster

Close under the ocean's surface lurked the sleek and sneaky *Metriorhynchus*, ready to attack. This marine crocodile of the Middle to Late Jurassic periods had a streamlined body with few of the scaly bumps and lumps that modern crocodiles possess. Measuring about 10 feet (3 m) long, the animal had a long, powerful tail that propelled it through the sea. Fossilized stomach contents show that *Metriorhynchus* (which means "moderate snout") snatched up anything that strayed too close to its mouth. The carnivorous sea monster tackled the giant fish *Leedsichthys* and successfully grabbed careless pterodactyls in mid-air by leaping out of the deep. Its paddle-like feet and finned tail made it so well suited to sea life that it came on land only to lay eggs. Then the huge animal would have returned to the sea immediately, leaving its young to hatch and make the perilous journey down the beach to the ocean alone. Ironically, hungry, flying reptiles such as pterodactyls may have been waiting in the air to dive down and pick up *Metriorhynchus*'s vulnerable offspring for their dinner.

The Art of Flight

At the beginning of the 1900s, people all around the world were fascinated with flying. Orville and Wilbur Wright (pictured) had just taken their first flight in an airplane at Kitty Hawk, North Carolina, in 1903, and the interest carried over, even to the study of pterodactyls. Engineers and inventors of the 20th century regarded flight as the greatest achievement in the art of movement. They studied bats and birds in their attempts to build the first flying machine for humans. They also analyzed the lightly built skeleton, strong muscles, and wide wings of the pterodactyl. Scientists today at Texas Tech University are studying pterodactyls' bodies to design a new spy plane called the Pterodrone. Pterodactyls went extinct millions of years ago, but the newly designed plane will bring the flying reptiles to life, replacing blood and bones with carbon fiber and batteries. The unmanned, robotic spy plane is about the size of a crow, with a similar wingspan of nearly 32 inches (81 cm). It is designed to fly, sail, and land in hard-to-reach places to gather information.